D1710699

Disappearing Acts

Emerald Boas
Rain Forest Undercover

by Catherine Nichols

Consultant: Raoul Bain
American Museum of Natural History
New York, New York

BEARPORT
PUBLISHING

NEW YORK, NEW YORK

Credits

Cover, © Hannamariah/Shutterstock, and Morely Read/iStockphoto; TOC, © fivespots/Shutterstock; 4–5, © Jany Sauvanet/Photo Researchers, Inc.; 7, © Gerry Ellis/Minden Pictures; 9, © Juniors Bildarchiv/Alamy; 11, © BIOS Bios - Auteurs (droits gérés) Montford Thierry / Peter Arnold Inc.; 12, © Pete Oxford/Nature Picture Library; 13, © NHPA/Photoshot; 14T, © Dr. Morley Read/Shutterstock; 14M, © Luiz C. Marigo/Peter Arnold Inc.; 14B, © Warwick Lister-Kaye/iStockphoto; 15, © Nick Gordon/Ardea; 16, © Jany Sauvanet/Photo Researchers, Inc.; 17, © Pete Oxford/Nature Picture Library; 18, © Brian Kenney/AGPix; 19, © Brian Kenney/AGPix; 20, © NHPA/Photoshot; 21, © Andre M. Chang/Alamy; 22L, © Gavin Weston/Alamy; 22C, © Luiz Claudio Marigo/Nature Picture Library; 22R, © Peter Arnold, Inc./Alamy; 23TL, © Andre M. Chang/Alamy; 23TR, © Dr. Morley Read/Shutterstock; 23ML, © Hannamariah/Shutterstock; 23MR, © Dirk Ercken/Shutterstock; 23BL, © Jany Sauvanet/Photo Researchers, Inc.; 23BKG, © Eric Isselée/Shutterstock.

Publisher: Kenn Goin
Senior Editor: Lisa Wiseman
Creative Director: Spencer Brinker
Design: Kim Jones
Photo Researcher: Picture Perfect Professionals, LLC

Library of Congress Cataloging-in-Publication Data

Nichols, Catherine.
  Emerald boas : rain forest undercover / by Catherine Nichols.
    p. cm. —(Disappearing acts)
  Includes bibliographical references and index.
  ISBN-13: 978-1-936087-41-9 (library binding)
  ISBN-10: 1-936087-41-3 (library binding)
  1. Tree boas—Juvenile literature. 2. Camouflage (Biology) —Juvenile literature. I. Title.
  QL666.O63N53 2010
  597.96'7—dc22
                    2009039446

For more information, write to Bearport Publishing Company, Inc., 101 Fifth Avenue, Suite 6R, New York, New York 10003. Printed in the United States of America in North Mankato, Minnesota.

112009
090309CGC

10 9 8 7 6 5 4 3 2 1

Contents

Hide and Seek

A **rain forest** is filled with many trees that are covered with green, leafy branches.

Look closely, though.

Hidden among the trees' green leaves is something else—a kind of snake called an emerald boa.

The emerald boa's bright green **scales** and zigzag stripes act as **camouflage**, making the snake hard to spot in the rain forest.

A Leafy Home

The emerald boa is found in South America.

It spends most of its life in trees.

It hunts, eats, and sleeps in the leafy branches.

In its home, the snake is almost invisible.

Emerald boas are also called emerald tree boas.

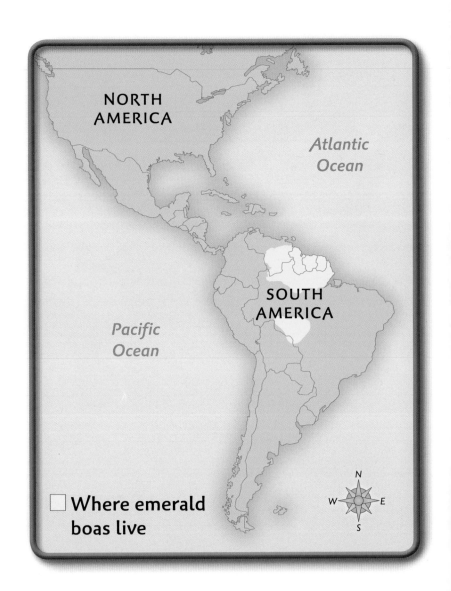

NORTH AMERICA

Atlantic Ocean

SOUTH AMERICA

Pacific Ocean

☐ Where emerald boas live

N W E S

In a Loop

During the day, the emerald boa doesn't move around much.

It stays mostly in one place, with its thick body **coiled** several times around a branch.

The snake's head rests in the center of its loops.

Curled up this way, the green snake blends in with the leaves on the trees.

loops

head

An emerald boa can stay in the same position for long periods of time.

A Nursery in a Tree

Emerald boas almost never come down to the ground.

Female boas even have their babies in trees.

The mother emerald boa gives birth to between 10 and 20 live babies once every two years.

The baby snakes are not born bright green like their mother.

They are either dark red or orange.

Female boas don't take care of their babies. Luckily, from birth, the baby snakes are ready to live on their own.

Growing Up, Growing Green

Young emerald boas start to change color when they are about four months old.

At first, only flecks of green show up on their scales.

By the time they are one year old, however, the boas are the same color as their parents.

Now bright green, the snakes are able to disappear into their surroundings.

green flecks

When an emerald boa is first born, it is less than one foot (.3 m) long. A fully grown snake reaches a length of about six feet (1.8 m) from head to tail.

Night Hunters

When night falls, the emerald boa is ready to hunt.

The snake lowers its head off the tree branch until it hangs straight down, pointing toward the ground.

In the dark, the snake stays very still, waiting for its next victim.

Emerald boas hunt mice and other rodents that live in trees. They also eat bats, lizards, opossums, and birds.

mouse

bats

lizard

emerald boa
hunting

A Powerful Squeeze

Animals scurry past the hanging snake without seeing it.

When one gets too close, the snake grabs it with its sharp teeth.

Then, still hanging from the branch, the boa wraps its body around its **prey**.

It squeezes tightly until the animal can't breathe and dies.

emerald boa squeezing an opossum

The emerald boa has very large teeth that curve backward, making it hard for prey to escape its bite.

Jaws Wide Open

An emerald boa does not chew its food.

Instead, it swallows its prey whole.

The snake simply opens its jaws and swallows the animal headfirst.

An emerald boa can eat prey that is bigger than its own body. How? The snake's jaws are loosely connected, allowing it to open its mouth very wide.

emerald boa
swallowing a
mouse

19

A Lazy Life

After its meal, the emerald boa might not need to eat again for a week or longer.

Now full, the snake once again loops itself around a branch.

Safe in its leafy home, the boa rests until it is time to hunt again.

Although emerald boas hunt many kinds of animals, they have few enemies. One animal that does hunt the emerald boa is the harpy eagle. Luckily, the snake's green color helps it stay hidden from view.

harpy eagle

More Disappearing Acts

Emerald boas are not the only creatures that hide by disappearing among the trees they live in. Here are three more snakes that blend in with their leafy green homes.

Green Tree Python

Green Parrot Snake

Flat-Nosed Tree Viper

Glossary

camouflage
(KAM-uh-flahzh)
colors and markings
on an animal's body
that help it blend in
with its surroundings

rain forest
(RAYN FOR-ist)
a large area of land
covered with trees
and plants, where
lots of rain falls

coiled (KOILD)
wound around and
around in loops

scales (SKALEZ)
small, thin plate-like
parts that cover a
reptile or fish

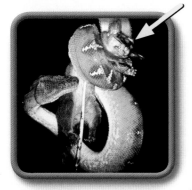

prey (PRAY)
an animal that is
hunted for food

Index

Read More

Landau, Elaine. *Big Snakes: Hunters of the Night*. Berkeley Heights, NJ: Enslow Publishing, Inc. (2007).

McDonald, Mary Ann. *Boas*. Mankato, MN: The Child's World, Inc. (1997).

Trueit, Trudi Strain. *Snakes*. Danbury, CT: Children's Press (2003).

Learn More Online

To learn more about emerald boas, visit
www.bearportpublishing.com/DisappearingActs

About the Author

Catherine Nichols has written many books
about animals and nature for children. She lives in
New York State's Hudson Valley with her dog and two cats.